SHOOTING THE STRAYS

ROSE M. SMITH

PAVEMENT SAW PRESS
OHIO   2003

Editor & Layout : David Baratier
Associate Editor: Stephen Mainard
Cover illustration: Rose M. Smith
Duck Logo: Joe Napora

Acknowledgements: Poems in this chapbook have appeared or will shortly appear in the following publications: "Shooting the Strays" in Pudding Magazine; "Cigarette Break" in Main Street Rag; "Weavers" in Concrete Wolf; and "Heirlooms" and "Summer Stalk" in Pavement Saw. Special thanks to: the Poetry Forum at Larry's and the poetry lovers formerly of Snaps & Taps in Columbus, and a smattering of folks at other venues throughout Central Ohio. To Jennifer at Pudding House, Steve, Lorraine, Scott, Is Said, Pamela, Ed, and Lloyd (Suddy): You are all first true friends. Thank you for your encouragement, your feedback, and your mentoring. You have helped in far more ways than can be named here.

And to my husband Jim whom I both love and cherish, who rescues me from the ogre that lives and breathes in some of these poems.

Pavement Saw Press
PO Box 6291
Columbus, OH 43206
pavementsaw.org

Products are available through the publisher or:
SPD / 1341 Seventh St.
Berkeley, CA 94710 / 800.869.7553

Pavement Saw Press is a not for profit corporation, any donations are greatly appreciated and are considered as charitable tax donations under section 501(c) of the federal tax code.
ISBN 1-886350-59-0
Copyright © Rose M. Smith 2003

Contents

Cold Deserts

Shooting the Strays

Weavers

Another Call from the Boss

Cigarette Break

Skinnydipping

The Switch

Coming to Bed

A Doctor's Word

Just Bread

Slow Order Cookin'

Concrete Geese

Amputations

Times for Believing

One Christmas Before Leaving

Heirlooms

Summer Stalk

El Shaddai

A Note from the Author:

Let it be our task to express with each poem a moment frozen in time: A moment's thought. A moment's anger or amusement. A moment's beauty, captured on a static white slice of consciousness and dressed in all the finery that particular, languid wandering of a poet's mind could muster as it waited for a passenger or stood in a grocery store line. What you say to a diseased leg. The crazed voice of frustration that wakes you on a bad day. The echo of old haunts now only remembered. The way the dying divest themselves of earthly goods. The way the elderly rehearse their failings over and over through their children's lives. These are the stuff of poetry. Not always happy. Not always sad. Not always archetypical, but always running in the soft ripple of common experience just beneath the words.

Cold Deserts

She called.
She made it sound like the whole thing was my fault.
I after all had been the one you said you might spend
some eternity with someday. I swallowed it-
swallowed it all like DQ chocolate malt with extra chocolate
one hot evening-cold menu served with soft, rich color,
just-right sweet, whipped into a swirl of
chilled delight to die for.

Three weeks before she came, they came.
Three knocks on my front door.
Three Feds but only one came in   politely   just to talk—
about the facts—that my car had been spotted
near a bank somewhere someone
decided to take down and they were, after all,
interviewing several auto owners,
not just me. I must not have looked like the
Bonnie and Clyde type back then,
all dressed in my cute little
day-job suit and spooning the last
of my medium Wendy's Frosty-fancy that.

I have pictures of you in the closet
in albums yellowed by gravity,
time, and sticky summer heat.
Now and then I pull them out
come close to your face again and search for clues.
Sometimes I swear I see a hidden mystery
in the shine of your left eye
the night that Pearce came through
with Jerry, Linda and Alvin and we all
sat around inventing conversation while we watched
Linda doin' shots
and Jerry doin' something strange with a cigarette
and watched traffic air brush orbs of light
in the rain on Livingston Avenue
through the fading
white sheers of my apartment window.

You are buried with all my other sins
in grown over waste places.
I try to recall how tall
you were, how sexy or how loud,
or how your black hair looked—all permed,
in that coiffure, doin' that Ron O' Neal, The Mack,
Superfly sort of thing without the cash,
but all I can remember is your mother's voice,
saying without saying
whether I knew what you were up to or did not
I may as well myself have pulled the trigger that
sent you home.

And all those chocolate malts are buried
in the broad expanse of these new hips of mine.
I longed for them back then, purchased them
with the best sweet moments of life.
Now here they are upon me,
lingering on for years like a soft, cold thought.

Shooting the Strays

Today they are shooting the strays at Kangirsuk.
Angels of mercy hold hot deliverance with both hands
to cull the crop of canine indiscretions
in Inuit villages nestled in the North.

I am reminded of dilation and curettage,
saline solutions, partial-birth removal
of smaller, much more human problems
before nuisances can be born,
before they gather in groups at daylight,
roam in packs at dusk,
hustle up to hilltops, street corners late at night
to howl like some ancestor at the faintest moon.

To the North, the Inuit slowly yield to protest,
agree to neuter sources they think that they own,
shield their eyes from the culling,
avoid the faces of rifled men,
preferring they remain unknown.

Here we pass anonymous
protestors gathered near the angels' gates,
oblivious of gunfire ringing through Arctic wilds,
of the yelp and hush of last breath, absence of breath,
the second screams of those who fail to die quickly,
the sharpening of knives to harvest what remains.

Weavers

To the tune of countless drums
the ancient chant
rumbles into your good night,
winds its fingers idly
into your moist gray;
leaves imprint and pattern
all along the folds you held reserved
for fonder memories.

Soundlessly, while you sleep,
dream catchers cordon off
reconstruction sites,
shuffle bits of definition
to unused places they have chosen.
Reshape the curl and fold of you
just enough
to leave you wondering
where you heard that tune before,
where you lost that one familiar fellow's name.

You rise to encores
spinning on your ceaseless fragile center.
You wake up singing someone else's favorite song.

Another Call from the Boss

4:30 a.m.
The you breaks through
the clay hillock of sleep
like dime store crystal shaken from the mantel
and I wake to the urge to offer up
prayer number 179 for your deliverance.
I struggle over the waterbed's edge
down onto pregnant knees,
lean into folded hands, release
the unutterable cry of one
who's lost the power of normal conversation.

I think of you a year ago.
Your robotic growl
pushed a language indiscernible
through the receiver straight into my fear.
I hung up on you.
You called again.
I listened immobile
while the balled wire of your sound
unraveled itself over the line.
You formed my name across a metal larynx
some therapist told you you could use
to make real words.
You called again and practiced,
repeating my name, familiar phrases,
everyday greetings, over and over
over the length from phone to cord to phone.

Today, I rise from dimpled knees,
arrive at work to find
your eulogy waiting in my voice mail,
some unfamiliar language of acceptance in
your wife's rehearsed announcement.
I play it, then play it again
before I hear
echo through the thick clay sound—
you in the dark of 4:30 a.m.,
you at the handset dialing,

you learning the finer art
of greetings in the distance.
I am amazed that you still trusted me
to recognize the newfound language
you had only then begun to speak.

Cigarette Break

Edwinna asks often how I quit.
She dons her coat each day
mid-morning at the office,
rummages through her bag
for tucked away delight
and pops "Back in a few ..."
into the auto-response line
of her Internet chat software.
We almost collide
at the corner once again.

I can remember the dizzying rush
of pulmonary chambers
feeling the spent smoke of a long dead leaf
fill and stifle the moist membrane,
trips on tiptoe into the dark
of grandmother's basement
to hold Forbidden firm between my fingers,
teach him to glow, to heat, to burn,
to draw his sweet cologne
into my young chest again.

I see the tamped, gray, dusty butt
of a Salem Light 100
balanced as if long practiced
between index and finger two
of my two-year-old daughter's
soft, splayed hand. I watch her
draw the discarded filter end closer,
closer to the mouth of innocence:

The slight tilt of her head.
The narrow, not shut fixture of her eyes.
A voice across time one again breaking silence:
*Now you tell her why she can't
do that.*

Edwinna asks, and I hesitate,
Recount for her promises whispered over
daily chore and routine: of thanking
unseen champions for deliverance
out of the hand of Habit—you know,
of prayer—of three days into a summer retreat
on a hill in Bremen, Ohio,
finding I had not had, had not wanted
a cigarette since.

She hears the name of Jesus—
this Jesus thing. This incongruous restraint
she thinks I have endured.
Her eyes glaze on a distant
point of focus.
She stares into a picture I cannot imagine,
then at me as if I'm from a planet not yet named.
She does not want to hear it but I know that
she will ask me how I quit again.

They give them such inviting names:
Marlboro, Merit, Virginia Slims, Kool, and One.
I suspect her brand is Black & Mild,
a wrapper dark, inviting, different, curious,
a wild leaf on the inside
refusing to be tamed.

Skinnydipping

Uncle Gene went,
but someone shot him in the night,
took him by surprise turning a corner
into his own room.

Then grandfather, too (but he was old)
and Jill, the girl I knew in school
who donned the veil and moved to California
just months before her body
unveiled
long held deadly secret schisms
waiting to be born.

This dude I met only that once is—
you know, dead
like so many foxes, Bambies
trapped in the sight of a hunter's gun.

Everyone falls into it
like that huge hole in the road
you cannot miss, can't drive around.
Some will take the high dive
one too many times in
then listen from a distance as the pall comes.

Wayne went home and measured out
a swift smooth stretch for his approach,
swept past us in a flurry then dove
right over the cavern's edge and
left us staring
one split second into eternity
while we all fastened tightly onto lifelines
in his breeze.

He taunts us from corners that light fails to reach
and never answers any of our questions.

The Switch

Frank took a fresh branch
from the neighbor's privet hedge—
slow growing bushes lining the alley
all the way to Ellen's house—
peeled away the bark of all his fury,
and lay in wait to see us turn the corner after dark.
Not truly dark, but overdue
by too much then for dark to make a difference.

We had stayed all day in Ellen's garage,
mixed the potion carefully:
catsup, jelly, mustard, sugar,
salt, milkweed and maybe mud,
each of us forced to swallow it
or do as Ellen judged.
She was older, bigger, therefore wise,
filled with a language few of us
could translate with mere words.

If you will show me yours, I will show you...

Boys with boyhoods cringing
but easy to reveal,
girls with absence, bare soft skin
where they imagined boyhoods should have been,
not a game to us, but a game to Ellen all the time:
our fear of tasting such sweet, sticky poison.

Frank took a fresh branch
from the neighbor's privet hedge—
green stemmed security lining
the alleyway to Ellen's house—
peeled away the guard in all his fury
and lay in wait to watch us turn the corner
after dark.

I do not recall the feel of my skin
tearing open with each lick,
but I do remember still the hedge.

Among the ruins and lasting scars
I find no privet hedge in all
that swept us into such swift circumstance,
but a wild branch growing
straight and tall
between the well-kept mounds of first intent.

Coming to Bed

Listening to the hollow wheeze
of your lungs' gentle labor,
the wail of many captured maids
fastened to steep cliffs and waiting,
warning uninvited breath away,
I dispel my fear they are the voice
of lurking, wanton ailment.
I have come to love these harmonic chords.

This single symphony,
so like an oboe's polished wail,
calling me close with baleful song,
tonal interplay:
he is calm, he is sleeping,
he is breathing, he is here.
The maple outside extends her reach
to shield you from passing headlights.
As they pass, I memorize again
the line of you, the luster of lids
that cannot hide the largeness of your eyes.
I want to kiss those eyes.
To my surprise, you moan and I
wonder who's pleasing you now.
You shift your bulk beneath
the simplicity of summer cotton,
reach across my chest to fondle my
chilled, exposed
arm.

This is timelessness and wonder:
Your hands quiet of their ceaseless preaching,
your soft exhale rumbling past my ear.
All my offerings tremble here and ripen
in your soothing breeze.
Awake and open, I imagine your salute.

Oh, what wonders we could make
here, at this moment,
if you were not sleeping.

A Doctor's Word
"There are treatments for this type of thing, but... she is so... obese." (April, 1994)

His lips curled carefully around the word
as though he were afraid
we had not noticed

the way the cool waves of her arms
lapped against our faces
when she laid us back in her beautician chair

or had not hear the floorboards creak,
the china cabinet rattle,
her own bones crack, complaining
when she walked by.

But we had noticed her open door,
her stalwart patience as she raised
her children's children
with hardly a harsh word.

We noticed her ever present peace,
her morning communions with Unseen Friend,
and the constant flow of wisdom
from her aging crystal stream.

She was a short, fat woman,
but certainly much more
to second generation issue
from her birthing place.

I realize he thought he might offend.
His soft dance left me wondering
whether he had really found
nothing he could do
or laid a wide berth
around her inconvenience:

afraid, despite his coffers full of remedy,
her inordinate size itself
might prove to be catching.

Just Bread

I come to you in evening light
rubbed with aromatics,
bathed in olive oil and
warmed by the heat
of another day's controlled oppression.
Laying myself before you, calling your name.
Call me Foccacia. I will go well with the soft fare
of Italy. Place an olive on my tongue.
You cringe and move away.
Such a wide loaf, too tough
to pull and peel, too coarse,
perhaps too natural, you think
but do not say.

I roll in coriander, cardamom
and strange herbs of the motherland
waiting to be used. They color me
the orange whisper of ambasha
and I wait in the night
for the soft rustle
of your feet upon the sand,
for the gray dawn at your back,
for you bringing home the product
of your stealth in far-off lands.
I awake to find you sleeping on the sofa
the scepter of your kingdom in one hand
the blue light from your many windowed watchtower
flashing indeterminate across a wide screen

and this is how we dance:
I close my eyes, imagine we
can meet here in this place of dreams.
I hold you in the foreign vision
of a woman you have not known.

You will take the prey—it will not matter
what kind, whatever spices there contained.
However long I marinate, roast, baste, bake or saute,
you will ask for it on Schwebel's—potato, if you please—
place it, press it between two slices
and love the soft yellow of their scream
because nothing else, after all, is bread.
Because anything pressed hard enough
becomes a sandwich anyway.

Slow Order Cookin'

They are
plucking the chicken you ordered
while you wait at Napoleon and Broad,
and Little Dude lookin' ten years old
with a Mohawk 'froin' his chin,
a strange shadow on his lip,
leans out to take your hard-earned from you
when you notice the newly-razed lot
where Kahiki had once been and you-
you want to stop, rewind your life
to high school, prom dresses, double dates
or new job lunchtime specials heavy
with Polynesian flair.
You want to wait patiently once again
for a table along the wall to watch
rainforests rumble their thunder
right up close—you still wonder
whether the plants were real.

They are probably cutting
the chicken you   ordered in good faith.
You realize this is where you first met
pineapple in your meat sauce,
or the best egg roll in the city
and met that friend for lunch when she came in
from Idaho and you wanted to impress her
with something close to home.
You want to dine again within close quarters
framed with greenery, cane and bamboo.
You want to taste again
cold noodles in peanut sauce
and watch it coax your hips into wider spaces
before cold noodles became the rage on every salad bar—
and that buffet, you want that grand buffet
'cause nobody   does it   quite   like   that   anymore.

They are probably breading your order
as you try to remember what used to grace this corner
before some non-commissioned southerner with a chicken dream
brought the bayou to this space, made this
the only place in Ohio
you could put one foot in New Orleans
and the other on an island somewhere.
And you shudder to think it's been a quarter century
since you first tasted that sauce—you learned
to long for tropical places
while you drove to Philly with the folks.
You returned with a couple of pounds you got for free
serving hot Bahama mamas to foundry workers
at Aunt Bessie's Chicken Shack
and your friends returned with tales of beach
and rich brown skins they'd bought in Florida—
which was okay 'cause you had eaten at Kahiki
and kinda knew what that was all about anyway.

You think of frozen imitations of once Kahiki food
and warmed over egg roll imposters
bought from the grocery store-and maybe
that old Polynesian god now stands in the back by the freezer
while they make 'em but you'll not easily be convinced.
Then you realize it's been six years
since you *last* tasted that sauce
and you want to go grovel, apologize
for staying away from distant cousins for so long.
You shrink in your seat 'cause it's people like you
who let old Kahiki go down, sell out to Walgreen's
and run.   You could swear

they had just started frying
that chicken you're waiting for
when the window slides back and
Little Dude with that *thing* going on on his chin
leans out to give you change and a Popeye's Chicken bag
and you think: *that few minutes waiting—*
wasn't quite so long after all.

Concrete Geese
(For Jennifer)

Thank you for the many-headed
contribution you have made to fill
that gully in the back.
It was kind of you to leave them
in triplets and in pairs
just outside your front room window,
just inside your pristine picket fence,
all along your sprawling garden path
alone, unguarded through the night,
and dressed in skimpy, feminine array.

You made me thankful after many years
my uncle owned the junkyard here in town.
He crushed them in his massive
press, collected them in his dump truck
and layered them in rounds like weathered onion
between the end of the Collins' yard
and the beginning of my own.

They have made a level place beneath the trees
fresh now with sod, thick and replete,
to while away summer evenings in peace.
No one would suspect in such a quiet place
there is a broken gaggle underneath.

Amputations

I have begun to love absence,
unwrapping, rewrapping the stump of it
with sterile gauze,
with elastic, flesh colored apology,
coaxing the remains of our excess
closer to the bone,
preparing the place you once held
for another not yet encountered or acquired.

When it throbs, I tell myself
it's natural to ache in this new place
where Division severed our foundation
round, exposed, and
clean as any ham bone's sad eyed grin.

When it itches to be touched,
I reach down to find you missing,
not even memory clear enough
to justify this shadow of sensation.

Nothing to touch. No place
to soothe the nagging reflex into silence.
Nothing to rub with a welcome hand
but this cloaked and narrowed ember
awaiting the prosthetic
like a child awaits a gift
of size and shape unknown.

I look down to find one limb
where two had always been:
Mine the ability to stand,
you the balance,
clear remorse to stand upon
whenever you were near.
Pain seeps through the fabric
like a simple stain upon the cloth,
and I realize I want you
but I do not want you here.

Times for Believing

Come on at full tilt sometimes, like this—
this flat tire on the interstate
on the side of a low rise mountain
just after 10 p.m.
in the seventh hour
of the trip back home from Heritage USA,
that brings you face to face with your
ignorance of how to raise the jack.
You always meant to find that
out, to memorize late
the things those kids in Driver's Ed
were taught for sure by pros
while you watched from the sad side of sixteen
and they each left you
shivering like a small girl
out in the cold of her own front porch.
You'd like to dwell on that
but your youth is immaterial
here on the steep black side of Mother Nature's
chilled back side as you
watch the lights behind you slow, pray
in the Holy Ghost,
and step out on the driver's side to meet this
red-robed
angel or devil, savior or
last man you will ever see
while cars whiz by at just enough an interval
to leave you shivering in the mouth of this great whole,
wolf meat in the treed descent
just over the rail.

One Christmas Before Leaving

Mama Gus memorized the cadence of our gaits,
gazed out of her second story window
to smile hello to each of us she had chosen, as
we carried our bags of burden
up the walk to rented doors.
All the street of town homes cradled Gussie's children.

She wound us around her spindle, one by one,
then wove our curious fiber
into the fabric of her own lengthy tale.
She brought us in to blanket her evening room
with our ideas of Christmas
and tucked us in small groups
around her evergreen of memories,
the popcorn, satin, velvet, tinsel, ornaments
mile markers along a century's path.

Take one, she said.
We hesitated, tenuously plucked
the gold gift box, the bright red drum,
the wooden soldier whose round legs
did not bend for marching,
the irreplaceable glistening cane,
the wood-carved waif you would not see again
on dime store shelves.

We accepted generations
from the abundance of her great tree—
each one a story turning about in our fingers,
Mama Gus watching the years disappear
into strangers' hands.

Heirlooms

I am baking this chicken in my grandmother's old cooking pot
oblong cast aluminum heirloom that hails from Sidney.
It was a gift from my uncle—yet another covered baking dish
from loved ones who did not know what to get her
for Christmas, Mother's Day, birthdays, other days.

There is a kind of trivet, oval, flat and full of holes,
that sits in the bottom to catch drippings,
but the trivet is gone.

I remember her using this pan once:

Uncle Bob brought her
a raccoon he and his buddy nabbed
in the woods one unusual day.
We watched her as she soaked him in the saltwater sink,
carved away the fat and pushed him
down into the pot, a bare dark thing with no skin.
We smelled his wild stench as she cooked him
and wondered if we would have to eat him, too.

Uncle Bob came by for a helping,
unsuspecting visitors were offered a piece,
and when the 'coon was gone, the Sidney pot
went back onto the top shelf of the cabinet
coming down years later as we sorted her belongings.

I wonder if she watches me
wasting such a pot on frozen chicken wings
and shakes her head at her little lazy one.
I am sure my Uncle would be laughing
at my choice of baking tools.

I would not mind.

When we sorted out the kitchen,
three sisters tending to unhappy chores,
I was the only one around who wanted it.
I was the only one around who also tasted the raccoon.

Summer Stalk

The last normal summer of the nineties,
before warm winter and drought
grasped us at the waist
three dizzying spins around the sun ago,
before the lawn won its protest
against redundant patterns
of heavy canine feet

one unremarkable fowl dispatch
left a poke salad plant outside the kitchen window.
I recalled many an unplanned stop
along a wooded road
to snip the point leafed wild stalk
at its hollow base—not the tallest,
but the waist high
plants still young enough for little hands,
no, not that one—that one.
Yes, pick that one. 'Atta girl.

She served the peppery mix
with cornbread in a shallow bowl.

Instinct set me into motion.
I plucked it carefully above the root,
rushed the precious stem inside,
left and whipped the Voyager around
to fetch fresh spinach from the corner store.
I simmered it slowly, a prize batch,
loneliness dissipating in its heat,
settled at an evening table
to travel back to memories refueled: it tasted

like someone had picked an inedible weed,
boiled it 'til its poison spread
completely through the pot
then fed it to me with a touch of
household cleaner for good measure,
and I realized
there are some memories
better left alone.

El Shaddai
(From the Hebrew: the mighty breasted one.)

the Breasted One
takes the nipple of his response,
and rolls it between the fingertips of power,
waits for the express demand of persistent people,
the high-pitched keen of intercessors,
the thought of them that causes
involuntary pulse and flow.

this stream
cannot be saved away in bottles:
this moment's answer
cradled in the mammories that wait,
engorged, discomfited for us and aching.
He lets down the answer long before we find
satisfaction at his massive spout,

expresses the excess carefully,
compassion a warm cloth laid across
the embodiments of answer.
the sweet cream of the lactate
runs onto the tongues of eager babes
grateful to take our places
while we root about in the arms of
surrogate, temporal supply.

In the distance, handmaids
of every colored robe and tapestry
approach the inner chamber at hurried pace,
bringing in the sweet offspring of other nations
anxious and instinctively seeking
a single feeding at his timeless breast.